ISBN: 978-0-692-00900-0

Created by Julie Jackson
Photography by Deryck Blake
Cover design by Lost Angels International
Revisions by Darby Printing Company
Interior design by Advantage Graphics & Signs
Brite Star Inc.
Printing done by Darby Printing Company

"Broke Jack's Light Taste Bud Tantalizing Meals"
www.brokejack.com
email: jjjackson@brokejack.com

BIOGRAPHY

J.J. Jackson grew up in Grand Rapids Michigan. She was taught at a very young age after losing her father to heart disease and kidney failure that healthy eating is essential to your well being, as well as exercise.

She is the mother of one son. J.J. takes pride in knowing with her help, many people have succeeded in weight loss. They also received from her the tools it takes to achieve a healthy lifestyle.

Ms. Jackson's goal with her new healthy lifestyle book "**Broke Jack's Light Taste Bud Tantalizing Meals**" is to reach as many folks as possible. This will allow her to give all the knowledge she has to help people get on the right track to achieving a healthy life.

For my Dad, the one of a kind W.E.J.   He is smiling down on me everyday… I miss you!! As a youngster, eating healthy was introduced to me by someone I've always looked up to and admired. I've used the knowledge you gave all my life.. Thanks Mom!!

Acknowledgments

Thank you D. Blake RPH in Atlanta, GA for all your support as well as L. Blake in Miami, FL for the sweet mangoes. My gratitude to Y. Ibraheem MS, RD, LD who worked so hard analyzing these recipes. You are the best!! To R. Goosby, in Los Angeles and M. Morgan in New York, thank you for years of kind words. Finally, I can't begin to verbalize how much I appreciate my family and friends who are always there for me no matter what. Love you!!

What's in this book?

"Broke Jack's Light Taste Bud Tantalizing Meals" cookbook offers healthy food creations for everyone! You will find plenty of color in each meal. The more color on your plate the healthier! Each meal is created to give you lots and lots of energy after eating.

In the second half of "Broke Jack's Light Taste Bud Tantalizing Meals" cookbook there are many helpful health Quick Tips.

Broke Jack wants as many people as possible to start eating lighter and healthier without much effort!

How was Broke Jack created?

Although many of us have experienced challenging times, I find a large amount of people call themselves broke who aren't broke at all. I don't know if its to keep certain friends and family at bay and far away so they can't ask for money, other favors, or it might just tickle one's tongue to say, "I'm broke." Because Broke Jack is a name most people can identify with, it will immediately grab one's attention.

Once the reader picks up "Broke Jack's Light Taste Bud Tantalizing Meals" cookbook, it will be hard to put down. You will laugh at the names of the creations in this book. People who ordinarily shy away from cooking and the kitchen, will get a chuckle out of preparing light healthy meals with such entertaining names. So let's get started cooking!!!

In less than a blink of an eye

Since the curious age of two, I've always been intrigued with the kitchen. In those days my mother was working at the phone company. One Saturday morning my father cooked his famous "Swinging Breakfast." It was me and my two brothers. My father left the kitchen for less than a blink of an eye. I quickly climbed onto the cabinet and found my way to the bacon he just cooked. The only problem was I had to reach over hot bacon grease. Somehow the hot grease splashed all over my little body. My dad rushed back into the kitchen coming to my rescue. Crying hysterically, he gently picked me up. In a panic my dad ran out the front door and down the street, even though he forgot his pants. He sprinted to the nearest hospital which was only a few blocks away. Dashing into the hospital door he sobbed uncontrollably not even realizing he was in his underwear. I guess one can say I learned the hard way… However with the love of my parents I survived. To this day I still enjoy being in the kitchen, but now I'm doing the cooking!!!

Testimonials

I never thought in my wildest dreams I would get so excited about cooking until I made Broke Jack's creations. I feel good about what I'm eating! I love the results!
K.Jones, Charlotte, NC

I'm a single parent of a teenage daughter and Broke Jack's meals have always put us in awe at our dinner table. Thanks for sharing your creations with us.
T. Scaife, Bufurd, GA

Broke Jack's food is the best I've had since my mothers! Try it and you won't regret it. I know my food!!
Thank you…
R. Goosby, Los Angeles, CA

Broke Jack's creations pulled me in the kitchen for good!! I'm cooking for everybody now!! Thanks to you!!
R. Ratteray, Bermuda

How to use Nutritional Analysis

Each recipe in this book provides a calculation of calories, total fat, saturated fat, cholesterol, sodium, carbohydrates, fiber, and protein in a serving. This information is a fair estimate for you to use in monitoring your intake and making food choices. Nutritional analysis is not, however an exact science; some variables cannot be controlled and other information may be overlooked or not take into account. For example, take a chicken recipe: All chickens obviously do not contain the same amount of fat; some are bred leaner than others. There are other questions: How precisely was the visible fat removed before cooking? How much fat remained in the skillet? How much fat was left on the plate? So don't get caught up in a lot of counting. A well-balanced diet that features fresh foods and follows clear and obvious methods to keep fat and calories low, will be the best way to go.

SECTION ONE: Locate Your Favorite Creation   Page 11

SECTION TWO: Quick Tips   Page 113

SECTION ONE

*BROKE JACK'S LIGHT
TASTE BUD
TANTALIZING RECIPES*

WAISTLINE REFORM

1 Tbsp of canola oil
2 lbs of chicken pieces
14.5 ounce can,(no salt added diced tomatoes)
½ cup (dry) red wine
2 garlic cloves, finely chopped
1 tsp of fresh basil
¼ tsp of ground black pepper
1 large red onion, chopped
1 large green bell pepper, chopped
1 large yellow bell pepper, chopped
1 Tbsp of corn starch
2 Tbsp of water
dash sea salt (optional)

Use a large skillet over medium -high heat, add oil, cook chicken until browned on each side until almost done approx. 15 minutes. Stir in tomatoes with their liquid, wine, garlic, basil, pepper, sea salt (optional). Heat until boiling, reduce heat to simmer, cover 18 minutes. Add onions and peppers; cover again, and simmer, add'l 12 minutes. While its simmering, in a cup stir cornstarch and water until smooth, slowly add to chicken mixture, stir frequently until thickened, chicken should be tender, when tested with fork. Tastes great over cooked brown rice. Serves 4 (serving size 1 cup.)

Calories - 429	Carbohydrates – 17 g
Total fat - 22g	Fiber 3 g
Saturated fat – 3 g	Protein – 42 g
Cholesterol – 193 mg	Sodium – 234 mg

PROFILE FABRICATOR

1 medium red bell pepper (seeded, chopped)
1 medium yellow bell pepper (seeded, chopped)
1 medium green bell pepper (seeded, chopped)
1 medium red onion (chopped)
2 cups of uncooked broccoli crowns
1 bag of frozen medium shrimp (14 oz)
4 small red potatoes (chopped)
2 garlic cloves (finely chopped)
1 Tbsp of fresh lemon juice
dash of sea salt (optional)
dash of white pepper

In a large pan add canola oil over medium-high heat add potatoes, cook 18 minutes turning frequently. Add pepper and sea salt (optional) while turning frequently add vegetables and garlic and cook an add'l 2 minutes, set aside. (DON'T OVER COOK VEGETABLES). Rinse off and pat dry thawed shrimp, return pan with vegetable mixture to medium-high heat and add shrimp continue turning frequently, add the fresh lemon juice. Cook until shrimp is heated all the way through approx. 5 minutes. Serves 4 ($1^1/4$ cup serving.)

Calories - 377   *Carbohydrates- 35 g*
Total fat – 7 g   *Fiber – 5 g*
Saturated fat- 1 g   *Protein – 36 g*
Cholesterol – 237 mg   *Sodium – 384 mg*

LIFELESS SPOUSE

1 ½ lbs fresh or frozen red snapper
1 large red onion (diced)
3 celery stalks (sliced)
1 Tbsp of butter or butter substitute
1 Tbsp of curry powder
dash of sea salt (optional)
¼ cup of 1% milk

Place the fish in a greased baking dish, large enough for fish and ingredients. In a skillet, sauté onions and celery in butter until tender, add curry powder and sea salt; mix well remove from heat, stir in milk. Spoon mixture over fish. Bake uncovered at 350 degrees for 20 minutes or until fish flakes easily with a fork. Serves 6 (eat with a green salad) serving size 1 fish fillet.

Calories — 155   *Carbohydrates — 6 g*
Total fat — 4 g   *Fiber — 1 g*
Saturated fat — 2 g   *Protein — 24 g*
Cholesterol — 46 mg   *Sodium 381 mg*

PRETTY RICKY

4 tilapia fillets
2 sweet mangoes (finely chopped)
1 red bell pepper (finely chopped)
1 yellow bell pepper (finely chopped)
1 medium red onion (finely chopped)
1 Tbsp of brown sugar
1 tsp of fresh lemon juice
2 Tbsp of safflower oil
1 tsp of dry jerk seasoning
dash of sea salt (optional)

Rinse off and dry the peppers and chop. Peel red onion and chop. In a large pan over medium-high heat, add safflower oil, peppers and onions and stir well. Cook 5 minutes, then turn heat off. Peel the skin off the mangoes, chop, add to mixture in pan. Add brown sugar and lemon juice, dry jerk seasoning and dash of sea salt (optional) turn heat back on, to medium, sauté 7 minutes, stirring constantly, turn off heat. Rinse off tilapia fillets, pat dry. Turn oven on 375 F, place fish onto large piece of aluminum foil, seal and cook 10-12 minutes or until fish flakes easily with a fork. Remove fish from oven, spoon mango salsa mixture over fish fillets. (Tastes great with asparagus) Serves 4 (serving size 1 fish fillet, 1 Tbsp of mango salsa)

Calories - 255 *Carbohydrates – 32 g*
Total fats – 8 g *Fiber – 4 g*
Saturated fat- 1 g *Protein 17 g*
Cholesterol – 38 mg *Sodium – 60 mg*

CHEAP BOSS

3 cups of uncooked (whole grain) elbow macaroni
⅓ cup of all-purpose flour
2 ⅔ cups of fat- free milk
1 cup shredded Swiss cheese
½ cup grated fresh Parmesan cheese
1 cup shredded extra sharp Cheddar cheese
dash of sea salt (optional)
canola oil cooking spray
⅓ cup of crushed melba toast
1 Tbsp of butter, softened

Cook macaroni according to package directions, omitting salt and fat. Drain. Preheat oven to 375 F. Lightly spoon flour into a dry measuring cup, level with a knife. Place flour in a large sauce pan. Gradually add milk, whisk until blended. Cook over low- medium heat until thick (about 9 minutes), stirring constantly. Add cheeses, cook until cheese melts, stirring frequently. Remove cheese mixture from heat, stir in cooked macaroni and sea salt. Spoon mixture into a 2 – quart casserole dish coated with cooking spray. Combine crushed toasts and butter, stir until well blended. Sprinkle over macaroni mixture. Bake at 375 F for 30 minutes or until cheese is bubbly. Serves 8 (1 cup serving size.)

Calories – 350	*Carbohydrates – 42 g*
Total fat –11 g	*Fiber 2 g*
Saturated fat – 6 g	*Protein 18 g*
Cholesterol – 32 mg	*Sodium – 497 mg*

CONTAGIOUS OPTIMISM

1 ½ lb of boneless, skinless chicken breast
1 medium yellow bell pepper (seeded, chopped)
1 medium green bell pepper (seeded, chopped)
1 medium red onion (chopped)
1 medium zucchini (chopped)
1 cup of diced tomatoes (with juice)
1 tsp of sugar substitute
1 tsp of fresh basil
1 tsp of fresh oregano
dash of sea salt
dash of black pepper
canola cooking spray

On a cutting board dice the chicken breast. In a large pan over medium-heat, coat with canola cooking spray. Add diced chicken, cook 20 minutes, or until tender, turning frequently. Add all remaining ingredients cook an add'l 5 minutes, still turning frequently. (DON'T OVER COOK VEGETABLES). Serve over cooked whole wheat egg noodles. Serves 4 (1 ¼ serving size)

Calories - 89   *Carbohydrates -14 g*
Total fat - 0.69 g   *Fiber - 3 g*
Saturated fat - 0 g   *Protein - 8 g*
Cholesterol -17 mg   *Sodium - 84 mg*

COFFEE BREATH

3 green onion stems (scallions) finely chopped
1 lb lump crab meat (drained and shells removed)
1 (12 ounce) can evaporated fat-free milk
¼ cup water
1 (14 ounce) can low sodium chicken broth
2 Tbsp of butter substitute
1 small red onion (finely chopped)
dash of sea salt (optional)

In a large pot, sauté the onion in the butter until tender. Add the broth and water, simmer for 10 minutes over low heat. Add the milk, stir well, and fold in the crab meat. Garnish with the green onion slices. Serves 4 (1 cup serving size)

Calories- 274	*Carbohydrates -17 g*
Total fat – 7 g	*Fiber –1 g*
Saturated fat –1 g	*Protein- 35 g*
Cholesterol – 90 mg	*Sodium – 800 mg*

TIGHT WIG

8 cups of yellow cornmeal
1 can cream of chicken soup (low sodium)
3 cups of 50% less sodium chicken broth
3 cups of water
1 ¼ cup of chopped celery
1 ¼ cup of chopped yellow onion
1 ¼ cup of chopped green bell pepper
3 eggs
3 Tbsp of ground sage
3 Tbsp of poultry seasoning
2 Tbsp of black pepper
dash of sea salt (optional)

Prepare cornbread according to package directions. Once cornbread is completed, in a large bowl crumble cornbread; add all ingredients, omit eggs. Stirring very well, until all ingredients are combined. Then in a small bowl, whisk eggs then slowly fold into cornbread mixture (make sure eggs are completely mixed in). Preheat oven to 350F; pour the cornbread mixture into a large baking pan; cook for 45 minutes. Tastes great with poultry. Serves 6 (1 ¼ cup serving size).

Calories – 890	Carbohydrates – 177 g
Total fats – 9 g	Fiber –11 g
Saturated fat – 2 g	Protein 21 g
Cholesterol – 100 mg	Sodium – 700 mg

DESPERATE NIGHT OUT

2 ½ cups cooked angel hair pasta
(about 5 oz uncooked pasta)
¾ cup of chopped vine tomato
½ cup of chopped red bell pepper
½ cup of yellow bell pepper
¼ cup of chopped green onions (scallions)
1 Tbsp of chopped green olives
2 Tbsp of fresh lemon juice
1 Tbsp of olive oil
½ tsp of dried thyme
½ tsp of white pepper
¼ tsp of dried oregano
¼ tsp of dried basil
¾ pound of cooked medium shrimp
1 garlic clove, minced
¼ cup of feta cheese (reduce fat)
1 Tbsp of chopped fresh parsley
dash of sea salt (optional)

Combine the first 14 ingredients in a large bowl. Sprinkle with feta cheese and parsley. Serves 5 (2 cup serving size)

Calories - 252	*Carbohydrates - 27 g*
Total fat -7 g	*Fiber - 2 g*
Saturated fat - 2 g	*Protein - 20 g*
Cholesterol - 114 mg	*Sodium - 249 mg*

STALKING STEW

1 large cabbage head
1 large green bell pepper
1 medium red onion
1 (28oz) can of stewed tomatoes (or diced)
1 cup of beef broth (low sodium)
3 cups of water
1 tsp of sea salt (optional)
1 Tbsp of garlic powder
¼ tsp of white pepper
2 ½ cups of frozen carrots
1 lb of lean ground beef
canola oil cooking spray

Rinse off and pat dry cabbage and green bell pepper and roughly chop. Peel onion and chop as well, set aside. Spray a large pan with canola oil cooking spray; using medium-high heat; brown ground beef, turning frequently cook 12 minutes, or until done. Add garlic powder, pepper and sea salt (optional); stir and set aside. In a large pot add 3 cups of water, cabbage, onion; cook over medium heat until cabbage is tender; approx. 10 minutes; stirring frequently. Then add beef broth, fold in ground beef, green bell pepper, carrots and stewed tomatoes; stirring from bottom of pot; simmer for 20 minutes. Serves 4-6(1 ¼ cup serving size)

Calories - 182   *Carbohydrates - 24 g*
Total fat - 6 g   *Fiber - 8 g*
Saturated fat - 3 g   *Protein - 29 g*
Cholesterol - 70 mg   *Sodium - 502 mg*

CONVENIENT AMNESIA

1 cup of chopped summer squash
1 cup of chopped zucchini
½ cup of scallions (green onions)
4 medium red potatoes, chopped
1 cup cherry tomatoes, cut in half
1 lb of medium shrimp (peeled and deveined)
½ lb of sea scallops
½ tsp of dry jerk seasoning
¼ cup of sweet caribbean sauce
½ tsp of sea salt (optional)
canola oil cooking spray

Coat a large pan with canola oil cooking spray. On medium heat add potatoes turning on occasion, cook 10 minutes, add scallions, zucchini and squash also jerk seasoning turning frequently, cook 5 more minutes. Add shrimp, scallops continue cooking until shrimp is pink on both sides turning frequently about 5 more minutes. Add caribbean sauce, tomatoes and sea salt (optional), stir. Serves 4 (1 cup serving size).

Calories - 427   *Carbohydrates - 48 g*
Total fat 3 g   *Fiber - 5 g*
Saturated fat - 0 g   *Protein - 24 g*
Cholesterol - 213 mg   *Sodium - 461 mg*

NOSE FLARE

6 lb of small young collard greens
3 ½ cups of low sodium chicken broth
2 Tbsp of canola oil
1 large red onion, chopped
3 garlic cloves, minced
12 sun dried tomatoes
2 Tbsp of cider vinegar
1 Tbsp of brown sugar
1 fresh hot chili pepper (remove seeds, membranes)
½ tsp of ground pepper
dash of sea salt (optional)

Pick through greens thoroughly, remove any yellow leaves. Cut off thick stems, rinse several times in water. Pat dry, stack and roll greens into cigar shapes, slice into thin strips. Place greens and broth in a large pot, bring to a gentle boil. Reduce heat to simmer, cook 45 minutes, stirring frequently from the bottom of the pot. In another large skillet on medium-high heat, add canola oil and onion, sauté 4 minutes, add garlic and sauté an add'l 2 minutes. Add tomatoes, vinegar, brown sugar, hot chili pepper, sea salt (optional) and black pepper; sauté 5 more minutes, set aside. Greens should be all most tender, if so stir in tomato mixture, simmer for 30 more minutes, stirring frequently. Remove from heat cover tightly and let sit 20 minutes before serving. Tastes great with corn bread. Serves 8 (1 ½ cup serving size).

Calories - 135	*Carbohydrates - 6 g*
Total fat - 4g	*Fiber - 3 g*
Saturated fat - 0 g	*Protein - 5 g*
Cholesterol - 0 mg	*Sodium - 440 mg*

2 MINUTE MAN

10 oz package of romaine lettuce
¾ cup of light caesar salad dressing
4 boneless, skinless chicken breasts
1 cup of garlic croutons
½ cup of freshly grated parmesan cheese
½ cup of turkey bacon bits
canola cooking spray

Rinse off and pat dry the chicken breast, cut into bite size pieces. In a large pan coat with canola cooking spray. Over medium heat add the chicken breast. Cook 20 minutes, turning frequently. In a large bowl combine romaine lettuce and dressing, coat well. Add chicken, parmesan cheese and top with turkey bacon bits, also croutons. Serves 4(2 cup serving size)

Calories – 534	*Carbohydrates - 21 g*
Total fat - 19 g	*Fiber - 4 g*
Saturated fat - 7 g	*Protein - 64 g*
Cholesterol - 181 mg	*Sodium - 420 mg*

DIVORCE CELEBRATION

1 lb of fresh medium shrimp, peeled and deveined
2 lb of fresh crab legs
10 ears of corn (small to medium)
8 small red potatoes, cut in half
1 Tbsp of sea food seasoning
1 large red onion, chopped
2 lobster tails
fresh lemon juice, to taste

In a large pot, add 2 quarts of water, add potatoes, cook uncovered for 10 minutes. Add onion, seafood seasoning and corn, cook an additional 5 minutes, then add shrimp, crab legs, and lobster tails. Cook uncovered 10-12 minutes or until potatoes and corn are tender and shrimp is pink. Sprinkle with fresh lemon juice. Serves 4 (distribute equally)

Calories - 249   *Carbohydrates - 38 g*
Total fat - 2 g   *Fiber - 4 g*
Saturated fat - 0 g   *Protein - 23 g*
Cholesterol - 338 mg   *Sodium - 640 mg*

BLIND DATE

6 cups of shredded romaine lettuce
1 large tomato, chopped
½ cup of fat-free sour cream
½ cup of shredded cheddar cheese, reduce fat
½ cup of red onion, chopped
½ lb of lean ground beef
½ lb of lean ground turkey
6 white corn tortillas
1 Tbsp of hot sauce
2 Tbsp safflower or canola oil
1 Tbsp of fresh lemon juice
1 dash of sea salt

In a large nonstick pan over medium-high heat add ground beef and ground turkey cook until brown all the way through turning frequently, approx. 15 minutes. Sprinkle a dash of sea salt on the meat. Then cook corn tortillas according to package directions (can use the oil in the recipe to fry tortillas). Place tortillas on a flat surface spoon on cooked meat, onions, sour cream, lettuce, tomatoes, sprinkle with the lemon juice, hot sauce and cheese. Serves 6 (1 taco serving size).

Calories - 346   Carbohydrates - 21 g
Total fat -19 g   Fiber - 3 g
Saturated fat - 4 g   Protein - 21 g
Cholesterol - 67 mg   Sodium - 271 mg

ECONOMY TKO

2 (15oz) cans white beans, drained
1 small red onion, finely chopped
3 celery stalks, thinly sliced
¼ cup finely chopped green onion (scallions)
¼ cup red bell pepper, finely chopped
½ cup finely chopped parsley
2 Tbsp balsamic vinegar
1 Tbsp olive oil
dash of ground white pepper
dash of sea salt (optional)

Combine all ingredients in the order given. Add more balsamic vinegar if desired. Refrigerate until ready to serve. (eat with whole grain rolls if desired). Serves 4 (1 cup serving size).

Calories - 167   *Carbohydrates - 28 g*
Total fat - 3 g   *Fiber - 5 g*
Saturated fat - 0 g   *Protein - 9 g*
Cholesterol - 0 mg   *Sodium - 188 mg*

LAUGHING AND LYING

½ cup chopped green onion (scallions)
½ tsp of hot pepper sauce
2 cans of cannellini beans
2 cans of chopped green chilies (don't drain)
2 garlic cloves, minced
2 cups of red onion (finely chopped)
½ cup of fresh cilantro
1 cup of shredded monterey jack cheese
14 ounce can of fat free- low sodium-chicken broth
1 cup of water
1 tsp of ground coriander
½ tsp of dried oregano
2 tsp of ground cumin
2 lb of skinless, boneless chicken breast, cubed
dash of sea salt (optional) canola cooking spray

Heat a large nonstick skillet over medium-high heat coat with canola cooking spray. Add chicken to pan; cook until chicken is cooked all the way through stirring frequently, approx. 15 minutes. Add garlic and red onion sauté 2 minutes, stir in cumin, oregano and coriander, sea salt (optional) sauté 1 minute. Stir in chilies, reduce heat to low, cook 10 minutes. Add 1 cup water the beans and broth, stirring well. Cover, simmer 10 minutes, stir in hot sauce. Spoon into bowls, sprinkle with cheese, cilantro and green onions. Serves 6 (1 cup serving size)

Calories - 233	*Carbohydrates - 12 g*
Total fat - 6 g	*Fiber - 4 g*
Saturated fat - 3 g	*Protein - 33 g*
Cholesterol - 78 mg	*Sodium - 694 mg*

ATTITUDE ADJUSTMENT

6 Italian turkey sausage links
1 large green bell pepper, chopped
1 large red bell pepper, chopped
1 large yellow bell pepper, chopped
3 garlic cloves, finely chopped
1 small red onion, chopped
2 Tbsp of olive oil
¼ cup of low sodium, fat free chicken broth
2 Tbsp of freshly grated Parmesan cheese
dash of sea salt (optional)
1 tsp of freshly ground black pepper
1 tsp of fresh basil
canola cooking spray

In a large pan, use medium heat, spray with canola cooking spray. Add turkey links, cook until done, approx. 15-18 minutes, turning occasionally, set aside. Take the seeds and membrane out of the peppers, rinse well and chop, also finely chop garlic cloves and red onion. Add chopped peppers, onion, garlic, basil, pepper and sea salt (optional) to pan with turkey links. Cook on medium heat 5 minutes, add chicken broth, cook add'l 3 minutes (don't overcook vegetables).Stir in olive oil. Serve over cooked spinach pasta, sprinkle with grated Parmesan cheese. Serves 6 (1 turkey link, ½ cup vegetable mixture = serving size.

Calories - 253   *Carbohydrates- 8 g*
Total fat - 18 g   *Fiber - 2 g*
Saturated fat - 3 g *Protein - 15 g*
Cholesterol - 49 mg *Sodium - 816 mg*

KICK TO THE CURB

1 lb of dry pinto beans
1 garlic clove (finely chopped)
1 red onion (chopped)
1 green pepper (seeded, chopped)
½ lb of smoked turkey
1 Tbsp of sea salt (optional)
1 tsp of black pepper
1 ½ quarts of water

Pour pinto beans in a large bowl, cover with water, let sit over night. The water will cause the beans to swell. Next morning in a large pot over medium-low heat pour 1 ½ quarts of cold water, also the pinto beans and all the remaining ingredients. Stirring on occasion. Add add'l cup of water if beans began to dry out while cooking. Cook until beans are tender, approx. 55 - 60 minutes. Tastes great over cooked brown rice. Serves 4 (1 cup serving size).

Calories - 545   *Carbohydrates - 73 g*
Total fat - 11 g   *Fiber - 17g*
Saturated fat - 1 g   *Protein - 38*
Cholesterol - 59 mg   *Sodium - 538 mg*

MIDLIFE CRISIS

½ lb of lean ground turkey breast
½ lb of 95 % lean ground beef
2 cups of canned no-salt added kidney beans
(drained, rinsed)
1 large red onion (chopped)
3 garlic cloves (finely chopped)
2 cups of canned no-salt added tomatoes
½ cup of no-salt added tomato sauce
1 large green bell pepper (seeded and chopped)
2 celery stalks (chopped)
3 ¼ cups of water
1 ½ tsp of cumin
2 Tbsp of chili powder
dash of cayenne
dash of sea salt (optional) canola cooking spray

Lightly coat a large pot with canola cooking spray. Using
medium heat, add the onion and garlic cook until tender,
about 6 minutes, stirring frequently. Add the turkey and
ground beef cook until brown all the way through, about 12
minutes, stirring frequently. Add the water, tomatoes, tomato
sauce, bell pepper, celery, cayenne, cumin, chili powder and
salt; stir and reduce heat to low and cook for 30 minutes. Mix
in the beans and continue to cook until beans are hot, about 5
minutes. Serves 4 (1 ¼ cup serving size).

Calories - 367   *Carbohydrates - 28 g*
Total fat - 17 g   *Fiber – 9 g*
Saturated fat - 4 g   *Protein – 29 g*
Cholesterol - 90 mg   *Sodium - 467 mg*

THE JIG IS UP

1 green bell pepper (seeded, chopped)
1 red bell pepper (seeded, chopped)
1 yellow bell pepper (seeded, chopped)
2 cups of chopped broccoli
2 Tbsp of canola oil
1 garlic clove (finely chopped)
6 small red potatoes (cut in half) 1 tsp of fresh basil
dash of sea salt (optional)

In a large pan over medium-high heat add canola oil and potatoes turning frequently, cook 18 minutes, or until tender. Add the remaining ingredients, cook an add'l 5 minutes turning frequently (DON'T OVER COOK VEGETABLES). Tastes great with whole grain dinner rolls. Serves 4 (1 cup serving size)

Calories - 328	*Carbohydrates - 47 g*
Total fat - 8 g	*Fiber - 7 g*
Saturated fat - 1 g	*Protein - 6 g*
Cholesterol - 0 mg	*Sodium - 80 mg*

SOCK IN THE JOCK

6 multi-colored bell peppers, seeded
1 pound ground sirloin
1 cup of fresh mushrooms
¾ cup chopped red onion
1 cup tomato sauce
1 garlic clove (minced)
1 tsp dried basil leaves
1 tsp dried oregano leaves
1 Tbsp of Worcestershire sauce
dash of sea salt
dash of freshly ground pepper
2 cups of cooked brown rice
½ cup of shredded part-skim Mozzarella cheese
canola oil cooking spray

Preheat oven to 350 F. Cut the tops off the bell peppers, remove the cores .Trim the stems from the tops, and discard. Chop the remaining tops; set aside .In a large nonstick skillet, combine the meat, mushrooms, onion, and reserved chopped bell peppers. Cook over medium heat until the meat is brown, about 10 minutes; drain off any grease. Add the tomato sauce, garlic, basil, oregano, Worcestershire sauce, sea salt, and pepper. Cook over low-medium heat for an add'l 5 minutes. Mix in the brown rice. Spoon the mixture into the peppers; spray 8-inch square baking dish with nonstick canola oil cooking spray, then place the peppers upright into baking dish. Sprinkle with the Mozzarella cheese. Bake for 18 minutes, or until cheese is bubbling and peppers are thoroughly heated. Serves 6 (serving size 1 bell pepper)

Calories - 242	Carbohydrates - 29 g
Total fat - 5 g	Fiber - 3 g
Saturated fat - 2 g	Protein - 21 g
Cholesterol - 45 mg	Sodium - 346 mg

GOLD DIGGER

4 fresh or frozen lobster tails (approx. 8 ounces)
1 ½ cups of water
2 garlic cloves minced
½ tsp of sea salt (optional)
dash of ground pepper
1 tbsp of butter (or substitute)
2 tbsp of fresh lemon juice
(additional butter and lemon juice optional)

Split lobster tails in half lengthwise. Pour water into medium baking dish. Mix garlic, salt and pepper, sprinkle over lobster tails. Pour melted butter and lemon juice on top. Bake uncovered at 400 F for 18 minutes or until lobster is tender. Tastes great with a green salad. Serves 4 (1 lobster tail serving size).

2 lobster tails equals:

Calories - 232
Total fat - 5 g
Saturated fat - 2 g
Cholesterol - 223 mg

Carbohydrates - 2 g
Fiber - trace
Protein - 43 g
Sodium - 775 mg

HOW DARE YOU

1 6oz package of wild rice
½ lb of halibut
¼ cup of low fat mayonnaise
¼ cup of finely chopped fresh parsley
1 ¼ tsp of red wine vinegar
1 ¼ tsp of fresh lemon juice
1 Tbsp of dry mustard
dash of fresh ground pepper
dash of sea salt (optional)
1 lb of cooked medium shrimp
2 celery stalks (diced)
½ cup of thinly sliced scallions (green onions)
6 large romaine lettuce leaves (or red leaf lettuce)
3 small vine tomatoes, cut into wedges
canola oil cooking spray

Preheat oven to 350 F. Cook wild rice according to package directions, drain and cool, set aside. Spray a baking sheet with canola oil cooking spray, place the halibut onto it and bake for 10 minutes. Let stand for 5 minutes, then cut fish into small pieces, set aside. Whisk the mayonnaise, parsley, vinegar, lemon juice, dry mustard, pepper and sea salt (optional) together in a small bowl, set aside. In a salad bowl combine cooked rice, halibut, cooked shrimp, celery and scallions, add the dressing to the salad and toss. Place lettuce leaves on plates, spoon wild rice seafood salad on top, garnish with tomatoes. Serves 6 (1 cup serving size).

Calories 250	*Carbohydrates - 27 g*
Total fat – 3 g	*Fiber 3 g*
Saturated fat- 1 g	*Protein – 29 g*
Cholesterol - 159 mg	*Sodium – 392 mg*

SAY IT AINT SO....

1 lb ground sirloin
1 cup of uncooked instant brown rice
1(14 ½ oz) can beef broth- low sodium
2 garlic cloves, minced
2 celery stalks, finely chopped
1 small red onion, finely chopped
1 Tbsp of chopped parsley
1 medium green bell pepper, seeded and chopped
1 Tbsp Worcestershire sauce
¼ tsp cayenne pepper
¼ tsp black pepper
dash of sea salt (optional)

    In a large nonstick skillet, cook beef, garlic, celery, onion, parsley and green bell pepper over medium-high heat until the meat is brown all the way through and vegetables are tender. Add the Worcestershire sauce, cayenne pepper, and black pepper stirring well. Add the rice, broth and water, mixing well. Bring to a boil; reduce heat to simmer, cover and cook for 30 minutes. Serves 4 (1 cup serving size.) Tastes great with a green salad.

Calories - 227   *Carbohydrates - 30 g*
Total fat - 4 g   *Fiber - 2 g*
Saturated fat -1 g   *Protein - 19 g*
Cholesterol - 40 mg   *Sodium - 388 mg*

MISTAKEN IDENTITY

8 oz of uncooked whole grain bow tie pasta (farfalle)
2 cups of cherry tomatoes, halved
¼ cup of chopped fresh dill
4 green onion stalks (scallions) chopped
16 oz bag of baby spinach
2 Tbsp of fresh lemon juice
2 Tbsp of cold water
1 ½ Tbsp of extra virgin olive oil
dash of sea salt (optional)
¼ tsp of black pepper
8 slices of smoked salmon, cut into thin strips

Cook pasta according to package directions, omitting salt and fat, drain and rinse with cold water. Make sure all water is out of pasta. Combine tomatoes, dill, onion, spinach, lemon juice, 2 Tbsp of cold water, olive oil, sea salt (optional), black pepper in a bowl, stir. Drizzle over pasta mixture, toss gently to coat. Top with salmon. Serves 6 (2 cups serving size.)

Calories - 206   Carbohydrates - 32 g
Total fat - 5 g   Fiber - 3 g
Saturated fat -1 g   Protein -10 g
Cholesterol - 4 mg   Sodium - 603 mg

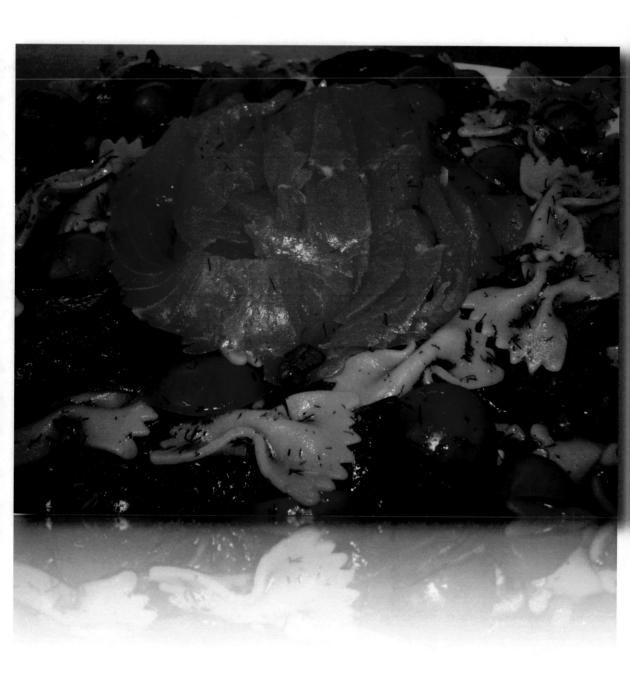

SO WHAT I'M BALDING

3 lb of boneless chicken pieces
2 cups of uncooked brown rice
⅓ cup of whole grain flour
2 cups of water
1 Tbsp of canola oil
1 cup of fat-free milk
1 tsp of poultry seasoning (low-sodium)
1 tsp of sea salt
½ tsp of black pepper
½ tsp of minced fresh parsley
canola cooking spray

Rinse off and pat dry chicken pieces, cover chicken pieces in flour. In a large skillet, heat oil at medium setting and brown chicken on all sides, approx. 10 minutes, turn heat off and set aside. In a large bowl, combine the next 6 ingredients. Cover a large sized baking dish with canola cooking spray, place the chicken and all mixed ingredients in baking dish, sprinkle with sea salt, pepper. Cover tightly with foil, bake at 350 F for 60 minutes. Make sure chicken and rice are tender. Sprinkle with parsley. Green salad optional. Serves 6 (1 ½ cup serving size)

Calories - 509
Total fat - 15 g
Saturated fat - 2 g
Cholesterol - 24 mg

Carbohydrates -156 g
Fiber -7 g
Protein - 22 g
Sodium - 680 mg

NEVER SAY NEVER

1 ½ lb lean sirloin (without fat, stir fry strips)
12 small red potatoes
2 cups broccoli crowns
2 cups grape tomatoes
2 garlic cloves
2 cups mushrooms
dash of sea salt
2 Tbsp safflower oil
canola cooking spray

Rinse and dry red potatoes, cut into cubes, heat a large nonstick pan over medium – heat, add safflower oil, and potatoes, cook about 12 minutes or until tender, set aside. Mince garlic cloves add to potatoes. Rinse and pat dry sirloin strips. In another non stick pan coat with canola cooking spray over medium -heat, add sirloin strips, cook until brown, about 12 minutes. Add sirloin strips, broccoli, tomatoes, mushrooms, sea salt to potato mixture. Cook add'l 5 minutes over medium-high heat (don't overcook vegetables.) Serves 4 (1 cup servings).

Calories - 215   *Carbohydrates - 22 g*
Total fat - 8 g   *Fiber - 3 g*
Saturated fat - 2 g   *Protein - 13 g*
Cholesterol - 36 mg   *Sodium -197 mg*

JUST GET OVER IT

4 cups of fat-free, less sodium chicken broth
½ tsp black pepper
½ cup of chopped carrot (medium)
½ cup of celery (1 celery stalk)
1 cup of uncooked whole wheat egg noodles
cup of shredded cooked chicken
dash of sea salt (optional)

Heat the broth, black pepper, carrot and celery in a 2 quart sauce pan over medium-high heat for 5 minutes. Stir in noodles, and chicken into sauce pan, continue cooking for 10 minutes or until the noodles are tender. Serves 4 (1 cup servings)

Calories - 103	*Carbohydrates - 6 g*
Total fat - 3 g	*Fiber - 1 g*
Saturated fat - 1 g	*Protein - 12 g*
Cholesterol - 35 mg	*Sodium - 600 mg*

IT JUST HAPPENED

3 Tbsp of all purpose flour
3 tsp of curry powder
1 tsp of sea salt (optional)
4 (6 - ounce) red snapper, or yellow tail fillets
1 Tbsp of butter, (or butter substitute)
½ cup of fat-free, less sodium chicken broth
¼ cup of mango chutney
¼ tsp of hot sauce (of your choice)
2 Tbsp of finely chopped fresh cilantro

Combine first 3 ingredients in shallow dish. Cover fish well in flour mixture. Melt butter in a nonstick skillet over medium-high heat. Add fish; cook 3 minutes on each side or until fish flakes easily when tested with a fork. Remove fish from pan; keep warm. Add chicken broth, chutney, and hot sauce to pan; bring to a boil, cook 1 minute, stirring constantly. Spoon sauce over fish, and sprinkle with cilantro. Serves 4 (1 fillet and 2 Tbsp of sauce = serving size)

Calories - 257   *Carbohydrates -14 g*
Total fat - 5 g   *Fiber - 0.5g*
Saturated fat -1 g   *Protein - 36 g*
Cholesterol - 63 mg   *Sodium - 386 mg*

THAT'S THAT

    1 medium onion (diced)
    1 (16 ounce) bag frozen cut okra
    1 (16 ounce) bag frozen corn
    2 (10 ounce) cans diced tomatoes, and green chilies
    1 Tbsp of butter (or butter substitute)
    dash of sea salt (optional)

In a non stick large pan, melt the butter over medium heat, then sauté the chopped onion until tender. Add the okra and cook for 5 minutes, stirring; add the corn, tomatoes and chilies cooking and stirring until the okra is tender about 10 minutes. Tastes great over cooked brown rice. Serves 4 (serving size 1 cup).

Calories – 130   *Carbohydrates - 27 g*
Total fat - 3 g   *Fiber - 5 g*
Saturated fat -1 g   *Protein - 5 g*
Cholesterol - 0 mg   *Sodium - 406 mg*

WHERE IS THE RING

3 green onions (scallions)
3 garlic cloves
1 Tbsp of ground allspice
1 Tbsp dried thyme
1 tsp cayenne pepper
½ tsp of fresh ground pepper
1 tsp sea salt
1 tsp grated nutmeg
2 Tbsp of brown sugar
¼ tsp of vinegar
¼ cup of safflower oil (or canola oil)
6 whole chicken legs

Chop the green onions and garlic. In a food processor or blender puree all the ingredients except the chicken legs. Put the chicken in a large pan and coat the chicken with the pureed mixture. Heat oven to 400 F, place the chicken in oven for 10 minutes. Take chicken out of oven and tightly cover with aluminum foil. Set aside for 45 minutes. Put the chicken back in the oven and then cook the chicken for 15 minutes on one side, then turn the legs over and cook 15 minutes longer. Tastes great with a green salad, or vegetables of your choice. Serves 6 (1 chicken leg serving size).

Calories - 184	Carbohydrates - 7 g
Total fat -11 g	Fiber - 0.46 g
Saturated fat - 2 g	Protein - 13 g
Cholesterol - 48 mg	Sodium - 446 mg

JUST BETWEEN ME AND YOU

4 - (6 oz) salmon fillets
¼ cup honey
2 Tbsp low sodium soy sauce
2 Tbsp of lime juice
1 Tbsp of Dijon mustard
2 Tbsp sweet jerk sauce (optional)
canola oil cooking spray

In a small bowl, whisk together the honey, soy sauce, lime juice and mustard. Marinate the salmon in the sauce in the refrigerator 6 hours or more (over night is ok). In a non stick skillet coat with canola oil cooking spray; cook the salmon on each side, approx. 5 minutes, until golden brown and just cooked through. Put the salmon on a large plate, set aside. Add the remaining glaze mixture to the skillet. Bring to boil, reduce heat to simmer; return salmon to the pan, spoon glaze over salmon. Serves 4 (serving size 1- 6oz salmon fillet).Tastes great with a green salad.

Calories - 273   *Carbohydrates - 19 g*
Total fat - 6 g   *Fiber - 0*
Saturated fat - 1 g   *Protein - 35 g*
Cholesterol - 88 mg   *Sodium - 400 mg*

AWKWARD SILENCE

1 lb whole grain Penne pasta
1 whole barbecued chicken (medium)
2 Tbsp of olive oil
2 Tbsp of white wine vinegar
1 ½ cup of cherry tomatoes
⅓ cup of chopped fresh basil leaves
⅛ tsp of sea salt
⅛ tsp of black pepper

Pull the meat from barbecue chicken, cut into shreds. Follow pasta cooking instructions from the package. When pasta is cooked, drain completely and transfer into a serving bowl. Combine the oil and vinegar and sea salt, toss while pasta is still warm. Add the chicken, cherry tomatoes, basil and olive oil to the pasta, and toss thoroughly to combine. Sprinkle with freshly ground pepper. Tastes better served warm. Serves 4 (1 cup serving size).

Calories - 640	*Carbohydrates - 85 g*
Total fat -16 g	*Fiber - 13 g*
Saturated fat - 4 g	*Protein - 39 g*
Cholesterol - 73 mg	*Sodium - 114 mg*

I TELL MYSELF I'M HAPPY...

5 garlic cloves (finely chopped)
1 medium red onion (chopped)
2 lbs of large prawns (deveined)
4 vine ripened tomatoes (chopped)
3 dried chilies, seeds removed (chopped)
¼ cup of canola oil
¼ cup of cilantro(chopped)
dash of sea salt (optional)

Heat the oil in a large frying pan, over medium heat add the garlic, onion, and chilies, stirring, cook 3 minutes, then add the prawns, cook an additional 4 minutes.(prawns should be pink on both sides). After cooking the prawns, stir in the tomatoes and turn heat down to medium-low for 2 more minutes, add the cilantro and stir. Tastes great over cooked brown rice. Serves 4 (1 cup serving size)

Calories - 344	*Carbohydrates -13 g*
Total fat - 18	*Fiber - 2 g*
Saturated fat - 0.73 g	*Protein - 64 g*
Cholesterol - 857 g	*Sodium - 60 mg*

LONG CONVERSATION, NOTHING SAID

6 tilapia fillets (4oz each)
1 lb of fresh trimmed asparagus
2 medium (vine ripened) tomatoes
½ tsp sea salt
½ tsp of fresh ground pepper
canola cooking spray

Rinse off and pat dry the fish. Place fish in a medium baking dish coated with canola cooking spray. Sprinkle with sea salt and pepper. Heat oven to 400 F, cook 10 -12 minutes or until fish flakes easily with fork. While fish is cooking, in a large sauce pan spray with canola oil heat on medium-high, add asparagus, sauté approx. 2 minutes (don't overcook). Rinse off, and pat dry tomatoes, and slice. Place fish, asparagus and tomatoes on plate. Squeeze fresh lemon juice over fish. Serve 6 (1 fillet serving size).

Calories - 119
Total fat - 2 g
Saturated fat - 0
Cholesterol - 50 mg

Carbohydrates - 4 g
Fiber - 2 g
Protein - 22 g
Sodium - 250 mg

FILE BANKRUPTCY, CALL IT A DAY.

6 whole grain English muffins
2 cups low fat pizza sauce
1 cup low fat mozzarella cheese
½ lb ground Italian turkey sausage
1 medium chopped red onion
1 medium chopped green bell pepper
canola cooking spray

Preheat oven to 400 F. Heat a nonstick skillet over medium heat. Coat pan with cooking spray, cook turkey sausage until brown, about 12 minutes. Place English muffins on a flat cooking sheet. Spoon pizza sauce onto English muffins, add onions, green bell pepper, cheese and cooked sausage. Place in oven until cheese is bubbly (approx. 8-10 minutes). Serves 6 (1 muffin serving size).

Calories - 364	*Carbohydrates - 40 g*
Total fat -13 g	*Fiber - 7 g*
Saturated fat - 8 g	*Protein - 23 g*
Cholesterol - 43 mg	*Sodium - 254 mg*

OLD MAN IN THE CLUB

4 Italian turkey sausages links (sliced)
1 can stewed tomatoes (14 ½ ounces)
1 medium green bell pepper (diced)
1 medium yellow bell pepper (diced)
1 medium red onion (diced)
1 can of low sodium chicken broth (14 ½ ounces)
1 cup of water
4 small red potatoes (diced) optional
1 tsp of garlic powder
dash of black pepper
dash of sea salt (optional)

Spray large pan with canola cooking spray; cook sausages over medium heat for 10 minutes. Add onions and bell peppers; sauté until tender, approx. 3 minutes. Stir in the potatoes cook an add'l 5 minutes. Add tomatoes, broth and water; cook on low-medium heat for 20 minutes, or until potatoes are tender, stirring to prevent sticking. Serves 4(serving size 1 cup).

Calories - 298   *Carbohydrates - 43 g*
Total fat - 8 g   *Protein - 18 g*
Saturated fat -1 g   *Fiber - 4 g*
Cholesterol - 37 mg   *Sodium - 723 mg*

SAVORY SLOP

4 (3oz) Italian turkey sausage links
1 large potato (diced)
1 medium orange bell pepper (chopped)
1 medium green bell pepper (chopped)
½ cup red onion (chopped)
½ cup sweet organic barbecue sauce

Spray a large pan with canola oil cooking spray, use medium heat cook diced potato until almost tender approx. 10 minutes; Add sliced turkey sausage cook 8 more minutes stirring frequently; add onion, orange and green bell peppers. Sauté an add'l 2 minutes (Don't overcook vegetables). Stir in barbecue sauce. Serves 4 (1 cup serving size)

Calories - 210   *Carbohydrates - 15 g*
Total fat - 7g   *Fiber - 4 g*
Saturated fat - 2 g   *Protein - 16 g*
Cholesterol - 70 mg   *Sodium - 480 mg*

BIG THINGS IN SMALL PACKAGES

Salad

3 cups cooked skinless, boneless chicken breast (cubed)
1 ½ cups halved red grapes
½ cup of sliced celery
2 Tbsp of sliced green onions (scallions)
½ cup diced red bell pepper

Dressing

¾ cup low-fat mayonnaise
2 ½ Tbsp orange juice
1 tsp curry powder
dash of ground black pepper

Combine all salad ingredients
Combine all dressing ingredients in a small bowl whisking until smooth. Mix the salad and dressing together. Serves 6 (1 cup serving size)

Calories – 273	*Carbohydrates - 10 g*
Total fat -12 g	*Fiber - 1 g*
Saturated fat - 2 g	*Protein - 27 g*
Cholesterol - 84 mg	*Sodium - 293 mg*

3 DAYS WITH THE IN-LAWS

1 Tbsp of Triple Sec
⅛ cup of Tequila
¼ cup of canola oil
¼ cup of fresh lime juice
½ cup of fresh orange juice
¼ cup of cilantro (chopped)
¼ cup of finely chopped red onion
½ tsp of curry powder
¼ tsp of turmeric
½ tsp of ground cumin
¼ tsp of cayenne pepper
¼ tsp of freshly ground black pepper
1 additional Tbsp of canola oil
1 ½ lb of fresh shrimp, peeled and deveined
2 garlic cloves, minced
dash of sea salt (optional)

Measure ¼ cup canola oil, lime juice, orange juice, tequila, Triple Sec, cilantro, garlic, onion, curry powder, sea salt, turmeric, cumin, cayenne pepper, and black pepper into a large zip-top bag. Seal and lightly shake contents to mix. Add shrimp to mixture and seal, making sure shrimp is well coated. Refrigerate for 1 hour. (Do not over-marinate)

Heat a large skillet over medium-high heat. Add 1 Tbsp of canola oil to hot pan and coat well. Remove shrimp from marinade, reserving marinade, and place shrimp in the hot pan. Cook for 1 minute, then turn the shrimp over, shrimp should be pink, do not overcook. Add the reserved marinade to the pan. Cook for add'l minute, then remove shrimp and keep warm. Continue cooking the marinade until it reduces to a thin sauce. Turn off heat, return shrimp to the pan, coating with sauce.(serve over cooked brown rice) serves 4. (1 cup serving size)

Calories - 436	Carbohydrates - 22 g
Total fat - 20 g	Fiber - 0.52 g
Saturated fat - 0.55g	Protein - 36 g
Cholesterol - 258 mg	Sodium - 253mg

AFTER ALL IS SAID AND DONE

¾ cup fat free sour cream
2 ½ Tbsp fresh cilantro
1 tsp of canola oil
14 oz peeled, deveined raw shrimp, rinsed well, patted dry
½ tsp chili powder
½ tsp ground cumin
2 garlic cloves, minced
8 - six inch corn tortillas
4 cups shredded romaine lettuce
1 large vine tomato, diced
2 Tbsp sliced black olives (optional)
1 Tbsp fresh lime juice

In a small bowl mix sour cream and cilantro. Cover, refrigerate until ready to use. Use a large nonstick skillet to heat oil over medium-high heat, add the shrimp to the pan. Sprinkle chili powder and cumin on shrimp, also the garlic, turning frequently. Cook until pink on both sides for just a few minutes. Remove from heat, dice tomato, shred the lettuce, add the fresh lime juice over the lettuce. Prepare the tortillas (using the package directions) Place the tortillas on a flat surface, sprinkle with lettuce, tomatoes, and olives. Spoon sour cream mixture on each, top with shrimp, fold and eat. Serves 4 to 8 (1 taco serving size)

Calories - 206	Carbohydrates - 21 g
Total fat - 4 g	Fiber - 2 g
Saturated fat - 0.5 g	Protein - 22 g
Cholesterol - 173 mg	Sodium - 308 mg

THEY'RE LOOKING, HOLD YOUR STOMACH IN!!

3 Tbsp fresh lemon juice
½ tsp of hot sauce (of your choice)
1 ½ lb peeled and deveined large shrimp
2 turkey bacon slices, chopped
1 cup of chopped red onion
¼ cup of chopped green bell pepper
2 garlic cloves, minced
1 cup of fat free, less-sodium chicken broth
½ cup of chopped scallions (green onions), divided
5 cups of water
1 ½ cups of uncooked quick-cooking grits
1 Tbsp of butter (or butter substitute)
1 tsp of sea salt (optional)
¾ cup of shredded sharp cheddar cheese

Combine the first 3 ingredients, set aside. Cook bacon in a large nonstick skillet over medium heat until crisp. Add onion, bell pepper, and garlic to bacon drippings in pan, cook until tender, approx. 5 minutes, stirring occasionally. Stir in shrimp mixture, broth, and ¼ cup of scallions. Cook 5 minutes or until shrimp is pink on both sides, stirring frequently, set aside. Bring water to a boil in medium sauce pan, gradually add grits, stir in butter and sea salt, stirring constantly until grits thicken. Serve shrimp mixture over grits, top with cheese and scallions. Serves 6, (⅔ cup shrimp mixture, ⅔ cup grits,2 Tbsp cheese, and 2 tsp of green onions = serving size)

Calories - 408   *Carbohydrates - 40 g*
Total fat -13 g   *Fiber - 2 g*
Saturated fat - 6 g   *Protein - 33 g*
Cholesterol - 246 mg   *Sodium - 890 mg*

JUST SOMETHING I THREW TOGETHER

10 cups of green leaf lettuce
1 medium red onion, chopped
1 small green bell pepper, chopped
1 large tomato, chopped
½ cup of low-fat shredded cheddar cheese
1 bag of frozen, cooked medium shrimp (14 oz)
4 Tbsp of light red wine vinaigrette
2 boiled eggs

In a large salad bowl add green leaf lettuce, chopped onion, chopped tomato, chopped green pepper toss with light wine vinaigrette. Place thawed shrimp on top of salad mixture. Sprinkle cheese on top, place sliced boiled eggs on each side of bowl. Tastes great with whole wheat crusty bread. Serves 4 (2 cup servings).

Calories - 218	*Carbohydrates - 10 g*
Total fat - 6 g	*Fiber - 3 g*
Saturated fat -1 g	*Protein - 30 g*
Cholesterol - 271 mg	*Sodium - 306 mg*

DOWN, BUT NEVER OUT

¼ cup of chicken broth
20 fresh snow peas
1 medium orange bell pepper (or yellow)
4 scallions (green onions)
¼ cup of chopped red onion
1 ½ lbs of sea scallops (small)
1 (28oz) can of diced tomatoes (don't drain)
1 tsp of dried basil
dash of sea salt (optional)
1 lb of fresh linguine (whole grain)
2 tsp of canola oil

Rinse off and pat dry the bell pepper, scallions, and chop into small pieces (add snow peas afterward) and set aside. In a large pan over medium-high heat add canola oil, chopped red onion and scallions cook for 2 minutes stirring frequently. Add diced tomatoes, basil and sea salt (optional) continue to stir, reduce heat to simmer, cook for 3 more minutes; turn heat off and set aside. Prepare linguine to package directions. Once prepared drain and fold into pan mixture adding chicken broth, snow peas; cook over low medium-heat for 2 more minutes. Slowly add sea scallops to mixture, stirring well; cook an add'l 4 minutes. Serves 4-6 (1 ½ cups serving.)

Calories - 664	Carbohydrates -102 g
Total fat - 10 g	Fiber - 13 g
Saturated fat - 2 g	Protein - 48 g
Cholesterol - 56 mg	Sodium - 331 mg

DISTANT LOVER

¾ cup of red onion (chopped)
½ cup of green bell pepper (chopped)
¾ lb of ground round
2 cups of no-salt-added tomato sauce
2 Tbsp of tomato paste
1 Tbsp of mustard
1 tsp of chili powder
2 tsp of Worcestershire sauce
½ tsp of sea salt(optional)
½ tsp of sugar substitute
½ tsp of dried oregano
dash of black pepper
12 (1 ½ ounce) wheat rolls, split

Heat a large nonstick skillet over medium-high heat. Add the first 3 ingredients; cook beef all the way through, should be brown, crumble beef in pan, with spatula. Stir in tomato sauce and next 8 ingredients, reduce heat to low. Cover and cook 15 minutes, stirring occasionally .Spoon beef mixture into each wheat roll. Serves 12 (serving size ¼ cup beef mixture, 1 sandwich.)

Calories - 202   *Carbohydrates - 27 g*
Total fat - 6 g   *Fiber - 3 g*
Saturated fat - 2 g   *Protein -10 g*
Cholesterol -19 mg   *Sodium - 392 mg*

BOOTY PRINTS ON THE COUCH

½ lb 90 % ground chuck
½ lb lean ground turkey
1 cup green pepper (chopped)
1 cup chopped celery (chopped)
1 cup red onion (chopped)
3 (14.5 ounce cans of no salt added tomato sauce)
½ cup of tomato paste
½ can of diced tomatoes (no salt added)
½ cup of water
1 tsp of dried basil
1 tsp of dried oregano
1 tsp of sea salt (optional)
1 garlic clove (finely chopped)
1 tsp of sugar (or substitute)
1 tsp of olive oil

Rinse off and pat dry green pepper and celery, peel onion. Chop all 3 vegetables (put aside). In a large nonstick skillet over medium-high heat add ground chuck and ground turkey. Fold in chopped vegetables, basil, oregano, sea salt (optional) and garlic. Stirring frequently, cook until meat is browned all the way through, approx. 15 minutes, turn heat to low. Add tomato sauce, tomato paste, diced tomatoes, olive oil and sugar. Stirring frequently, add ½ cup of water, stir well. Simmer 30 minutes (stirring on occasion). Spoon meat mixture over cooked whole wheat spaghetti pasta. Serves 4 (1 cup serving).

Calories - 365	*Carbohydrates - 32 g*
Total fat - 15 g	*Fiber - 7 g*
Saturated fat - 3 g	*Protein - 29 g*
Cholesterol - 93 mg	*Sodium - 502 mg*

WHAT YOU SEE IS WHAT YOU GET

½ tsp of dried oregano
1 ½ tsp of olive oil
½ tsp dried thyme
½ tsp sea salt
dash of black pepper
4 (6oz) tuna steaks
canola oil cooking spray
4 lemon wedges

To marinate steaks, combine first 5 ingredients in a small bowl, rub evenly over steaks, cover. Set in refrigerator for 20 minutes. Heat a large grill pan over medium-high heat. Coat well with canola cooking spray, add steaks; cook 5 minutes on each side or until steaks flake easily with fork.(don't overcook). Put lemon wedges on plate with each steak. Tastes great with a green salad. Serves 4 (Serving size 1 steak)

Calories - 250   Carbohydrates - 0.2 g
Total fat - 10 g   Fiber - 0.1 g
Saturated fat - 2 g   Protein - 38 g
Cholesterol - 63 mg   Sodium - 357 mg

TRAFFIC STOPPING SWAGGER

4 oz rock shrimp
¼ cup red onion (minced)
4 Mahi Mahi fillets 4oz
1 (5.8 oz) package wheat couscous
½ cup yellow bell pepper (chopped)
dash of black pepper
dash of chili powder
dash of sea salt (optional)
Canola oil cooking spray

Preheat oven to 400 F. Spray a shallow baking pan with canola oil cooking spray. Place fish in pan, sprinkle with pepper and sea salt (optional). Place pan in oven cook 12 minutes. While fish is cooking prepare couscous according to package directions. Spray a large pan with canola oil cooking spray; using medium heat add rock shrimp, onions, yellow bell pepper, chili powder and dash of sea salt (optional). Cook until shrimp is pink all over, stirring frequently; approx. 2 minutes (Don't overcook). Spoon shrimp mixture over cooked fish. Serve with prepared couscous. Tastes great with a green salad. Serves 4 (serving size 1 fillet, 1 tbsp shrimp mixture, ⅓ cup cooked couscous.

Calories - 423
Total fat - 2g
Saturated fat - 0 g
Cholesterol - 150mg

Carbohydrates - 58 g
Fiber - 7 g
Protein - 43g
Sodium - 394 mg

COMFORT

FOODS

SECTION TWO

BROKE JACK'S QUICK TIPS

Quick Tip

Move it to lose it! Physical activity has been cited as the most powerful tool for weight management.

Source: "Complete Food and Nutrition Guide" Roberta Larson Duyff MS, RD, FADA, CFCS.

Why exercise? All of your health problems will improve, or, you won't develop any. Every type of physical activity, from mountain climbing to sex, benefits your health. Exercise and food have a better effect on your health than any drug. Your overall quality of life will improve.

Source: Dr Gavin's Health Guide James.R.Gavin III, MD, PHD

Quick Tip

Excess weight can cause hormonal imbalances and inflammation that impairs the immune system's ability to fight infection.

Source: Prevention magazine, December 2009.

Exercise relieves anxiety and is a good way to work through emotions. It releases feel good brain chemicals, called endorphins, which are more powerful than morphine.

Source: Dr Gavin's Health Guide, James.R.Gavin III, MD, PHD.

Outgoing people are 50% less likely to develop dementia. Source: Karolinska Institute in Sweden.

Source: Prevention Magazine, September 2009.

Quick Tip

Burn fat all over, you could do hours of body sculpting workouts a day, but unless you add in cardio, like walking or cycling, you won't get the results you're looking for. That's because cardio blasts fat all over, showing off those shapely muscles. Aim for at least 30 minutes of heart-pumping, calorie-burning aerobic exercise 5 times a week. Source: Chris Freytag is a board member of the American Council on Exercise; Prevention Magazine, August 2009.

Lift. Weights, that is, women who pumped iron twice a week for two years lost more body fat and didn't gain as much belly fat as women who didn't lift, according to a study in the American Journal of Clinical Nutrition, *Source*: Health Magazine November 2009

Quick Tip

20% that's the percentage you can increase your energy level just by doing a low-intensity exercise like walking, according to a recent University of Georgia study, Researchers think such light workouts stimulate your body and mind, decreasing fatigue by 65%.

Source: Health Magazine; November 2009.

Get Happier! Depression is linked to deep belly fat, a study in the Journal Obesity reports. Make time to do what you enjoy, and talk to your doctor if you are feeling down.

Source: Health Magazine November 2009.

Quick Tip

GET HAPPIER, LIVE LONGER

Optimistic women are 30 percent less likely to die from heart disease, according to a new Women's Health Initiative study, so thinking positively is even more crucial as you get older. How do you make that a habit? Study author Hilary A. Tindle, MD, assistant professor of medicine at the University Of Pittsburgh School Of Medicine, recommends making time for simple pleasures like watching movies and planning vacations.

Source: Health Magazine, July/August 2009.

"Women who are hugged secrete higher levels of the hormone oxytocin, which relaxes blood vessels and lowers blood pressure," says cardiologist Nieca Goldberg, MD, medical director of New York University Women's Heart Program. *Source*: Prevention Magazine, December 2009.

Quick Tip

How do saturated fats affect my health? Eating foods that contain saturated fats raises the level of cholesterol in your blood. High levels of blood cholesterol increase your risk of heart disease and stroke. Be aware, too, that many foods high in saturated fats are also high in cholesterol-which raises your blood cholesterol even higher.

Source: www.americanheart.org;
American Heart Association.

Quick Tip

What foods contain saturated fats?

Saturated fats occur naturally in many foods. The majority come mainly from animal sources, including meat and dairy products. Examples are fatty beef, lamb, pork, poultry with skin, beef fat (tallow), lard and cream, butter, cheese, and other dairy products made from whole or reduced-fat (2 percent)milk. These foods contain dietary cholesterol. In addition, many baked goods and fried foods can contain high levels of saturated fats. Some plant foods, such as palm oil, palm kernel oil and coconut oil, also contain primarily saturated fats, but do not contain cholesterol.

Source: www.americanheart.org;
American Heart Association

Quick Tip

Cholesterol is a soft, waxy substance found among the lipids (fats) in the bloodstream and in all your body's cells. It's an important part of a healthy body because it's used to form cell membranes, some hormones and is needed for other functions. But a high level of cholesterol in the blood-hypercholesterolemia-is a major risk factor for coronary heart disease, which leads to heart attack.

Source: American Heart Association, www.americanheart.org.

Cholesterol and other fats can't dissolve in the blood. They have to be transported to and from the cells by special carriers called lipoproteins. There are several kinds, but the ones to focus on are low density lipoprotein (LDL) and high-density lipoprotein (HDL.)

Source: American Heart Association, www.americanheart.org.

Quick Tip

Trans fatty acids act like saturated fats, raising LDL blood cholesterol levels and potentially decreasing HDL cholesterol. That, in turn, may increase the risk for fatty deposits on blood vessel walls and heart attacks.

Source: Complete Food and Nutrition Guide, Roberta Larson Duyff MS, RD, FADA, CFCS.

Cholesterol is not found in vegetable oils, margarine, or egg whites, or in plant — based foods such as grains, fruits, vegetables, beans, and peas. *Source*: Complete Food and Nutrition Guide, Roberta Larson Duyff MS, RD, FADA, CFCS.

Research shows that soy may protect your heart, lower your cancer risk and build bone.

Source: Marisa Moore RD; a Spokesperson for the American Dietetic Association, Fitness Magazine, July/August 2009

Quick Tip

New danger fat: PALM OIL

As trans fats disappear from margarine, cookies, and other packaged foods, another potentially harmful additive is taking its place: palm oil. It was once lauded for a high vitamin E and oleic acid content, but research is turning rancid. PALM OIL IS LOADED WITH ARTERY-DAMAGING SATURATED FATS AND ACTS MUCH LIKES TRANS FATS IN YOUR BODY.

BOTTOM LINE

Stick to whole foods, and if you buy processed ones, pick those that have heart-healthy oils like olive and canola on ingredients list. - Paige Nestel *Source*: Prevention magazine, October 2009

Quick Tip

Men and women who limited their daily calories to 1,400 to 2,000(about 25% fewer calories than those who followed a typical 2,000-3,000-calorie western diet where literally young at heart — their hearts functioned like those of people 15 years younger.

Source:
Prevention magazine, study Author Luigi Fontana, M.D, PhD, associate professor of medicine at Washington University School of Medicine.

Fat is a concentrated source of energy, or calories. However, cutting back on high fat foods may not trim calories if too many carbohydrates or proteins take their place.

Source: Complete food and Nutrition Guide, Roberta Larson Duyff MS, RD, FADA, CFCS.

Quick Tip

Fat isn't just a lump of pounds- it's a biologically active substance that produces hormones like estrogen, which promotes tumor growth."The more fat you have, especially around the abdomen, the more estrogen you will produce, "says Sharon Rosenbaum Smith, M.D., Medical director of the Comprehensive Breast Center at St. Luke's Roosevelt Hospital Center New York City. Exposure to high levels of the hormone may increase a woman's chances of getting breast cancer over time.

Source: Fitness Magazine, November/December 2009.

Quick Tip

Basically, the term fiber refers to carbohydrates that cannot be digested. Fiber is present in all plants that are eaten for food, including fruits, vegetables, grains, and legumes. However, not all fiber is the same, and there are a number of ways to categorize it. One is by its source or origin. For example, fiber from grains is referred to as cereal fiber. Another way of categorizing fiber is by how easily it dissolves in water.

Soluble fiber partially dissolves in water. Insoluble fiber does not dissolve in water. These differences are important when it comes to fiber's effect on your risk of developing certain diseases.

Source: www.hsph.harvard.edu/nutritionsource/what-should-you-eat/fiber-full-story

Quick Tip

Soluble Fiber

- Oatmeal, oat bran
- Lentils
- Nuts and seeds
- Apples
- Legumes
- Pears
- Beans
- Dried Peas
- Blueberries
- Strawberries

Insoluble Fiber

- Whole wheat bread
- Barley
- Couscous
- Brown rice
- Bulgur
- Whole grain breakfast cereals
- Wheat bran
- Seeds
- Carrots
- Cucumbers
- Zucchini
- Celery
- Tomatoes

Source:
www.hsph.harvard.edu/nutritionsource/what-should-you-eat/fiber-full-story

Quick Tip

Foods rich in certain omega-3 fats called EPA and DHA can reduce cardiovascular disease, improve your mood and help prevent dementia. The best sources for the EPA and DHA omega-3 fats are fatty fish such as salmon, herring, mackerel, anchovies, sardines, and some cold water fish oil supplements. Canned albacore tuna and lake trout can be good sources depending on how the fish where raised and processed.

Source: www.HELPGUIDE.org
A TRUSTED NON-PROFIT RESOURCE

Some people avoid seafood because they worry about mercury or other possible toxins. But most experts agree that the benefits of eating 2 servings a week of cold water fatty fish outweigh the risks.

Source: www.HELPGUIDE.org
A TRUSTED NON-PROFIT RESOURCE

Quick Tip

Antioxidants are a handful of vitamins, minerals, carotenoids, and polyphenols present in a variety of foods that significantly slow or prevent the oxidative (damage from oxygen) process and so prevent or repair damage to your body cells. They may also improve immune function and perhaps lower risk for infection and cancer.

Source: Complete Food and Nutrition Guide; Roberta Larson Duyff MS, RD, FADA, CFCS.

A free radical is an unstable molecule with a missing electron. Free radicals can damage body cells and tissues, as well as DNA, your body's master plan for reproducing cells. Environmental factors such as cigarette smoke and ultraviolet light also cause free radicals to form in your body.

Source: Complete Food and Nutrition Guide; Roberta Larson Duyff MS, RD, FADA, CFCS.

Quick Tip

Probiotics improve digestion, constipation, and bloating.

Now research from Finland's University of Turku finds that Probiotics may also cut belly fat by altering how we use and store energy. Yet, according to American Dietetic Association, only 20% of Americans have heard of them, that's certain to change as companies roll out a new wave of products touting the gut-friendly bugs, giving consumers new ways to trim their tummies.

Source: Prevention Magazine, November 2009.

Eat enough calories by not too many. Maintain a balance between your calorie intake and calorie expenditure-that is, don't eat more food than your body uses. The average recommended daily allowance is 2,000 calories, but this depends on your age, height, weight, and physical activity.

Source: HELPGUIDE.org,
A TRUSTED NON-PROFIT RESOURCE.

Quick Tip

Most people have difficulty digesting lactose-the main type of sugar found in dairy products. People with lactose intolerance experience upset stomachs and diarrhea when they consume dairy foods, particularly milk. Fortunately, soy foods allow people with lactose intolerance to consume the required protein and calcium they need without difficulty.

Source: Super foods Rx; Steven Pratt, M.D; and Kathy Matthews.

Flax seeds are a rich source of omega-3 fats. They are an excellent source of soluble and insoluble fiber beneficial for regulating cholesterol, blood glucose, and digestion.

Source: "101Foods That Could Save Your Life"; David Grotto, RD, LDN

Quick Tip

"Try out oils" Besides olive oil, consider other healthy oils, such as wheat germ, flaxseed, and walnut.

They supply nutrients like vitamin E and omega-3 fats.

High heat can destroy the nutrients so lightly drizzle these oils over food for a nutty flavor. *Source*: Jeremy Bearman, executive chef at Rouge Tomate in New York City; Prevention Magazine, November 2009.

The omega-3 fatty acids in grilled salmon help prevent heart disease and boost brain power.

Source: Marisa Moore, R.D; a Spokesperson for the American Dietetic Association, Fitness Magazine July/August 2009.

Quick Tip

The darker the leaves the more vitamins and minerals. Try a spring mix of greens for varied textures and flavors. *Source*: Marisa Moore, R.D; a Spokesperson for the American Dietetic Association, Fitness Magazine, July/August 2009.

"Made with whole grains" The USDA does not regulate this value-added claim, which often appears on processed foods such as crackers, cereals, and breads.

Because labels usually don't indicate how many whole grains are included, this is a meaningless term. Instead, look for products that contain 100% whole grain, and read the ingredients list, which orders ingredients from most to least. Whole grain (wheat, oats) should be first, and enriched wheat flour -aka refined white flour should not be included at all.

Source: Paige Nestel, Prevention Magazine, August 2009.

Quick Tip

University of Purdue researchers recently concluded that a compound in green tea inhibits the growth of cancer cells. There is also research indicating that drinking green tea lowers total cholesterol levels, as well as improving the ratio of good (HDL) cholesterol to bad (LDL) cholesterol.

Source: About.com, Chinese Food

New evidence is emerging that green tea can even help dieters. In November, 1999 the American Journal of Clinical Nutrition published the results of a study at the University of Geneva in Switzerland. Researchers found that men who were given a combination of caffeine and green tea extract burned more calories than those given only caffeine or a placebo.

Source: About.com, Chinese Food

Quick Tip

Green tea is good for your skin and helps fight cancer. Researchers say it's even an effective belly buster. Researchers speculate that phytonutrients in green tea may help speed the breakdown of fat.

Source: Journal of Nutrition; Prevention Magazine, December 2009.

Vitamin B6 deficiency has been linked to anxiety, stress, and depression, women are more likely to become deficient in B6 as they age, according to researchers at the Jean Mayer USDA Human Nutrition Research Center on Aging at Tufts University.

Source: Prevention Magazine 2009.

Quick Tip

After olive oil has been stored for six months, its antioxidants are 40 percent less effective at fighting cell-damaging free radicals, the Journal of Food Science finds. Buy small bottles; store in a cool place.

Source: Self Magazine, August 2009.

Chronic stress could cause fat buildup, especially around your abs, an animal study in Nature Medicine Notes; it may cause your body to secrete a hormone that triggers the growth of fat cells.

Source: Self Magazine, August 2009.

People who get more of their calories at breakfast gain less weight than people who skip it or eat less. AM eaters have more stable blood glucose levels during the day, so they resist snacks better.

Source: Self Magazine, August 2009.

Quick Tip

Healthy eating alone certainly can't totally protect you from cancer, but it's one of your most potent weapons, along with avoiding tobacco.

Source: Living well expert Karen Collins R.D. Living Well; Montel Williams.

Since water has no calories, most people think it doesn't have anything to do with weight loss. But it does, and it's essential for good health. When you're dehydrated, your body's ability to perform virtually every physiological function, including the important process of fat metabolism, decreases.

Source: "Get with the program guide to good eating" Bob Greene

Quick Tip

Science has confirmed that the nutrients in our food can slow down and even reverse aging. When you eat well, the repair starts immediately on a cellular level, but some benefits take years.

Source: Tamas Horvath, PhD, a neurobiologist at Yale University. / Prevention magazine, September 2009.

Antioxidants, especially abundant in fruits and vegetables, are powerful compounds that cancel out cancer-causing free radicals before they damage cells.

Source: Hellmann/Prevention magazine September 2009.

Quick Tip

Research shows that consumption of vegetables and fruits high in vitamin C are associated with a reduced risk of death from numerous causes including heart disease stroke and cancer. *Source*: David W Grotto, RD, LDN; 101 Foods that Could Save your Life.

With the help of sunlight, a form of cholesterol in your skin can change to vitamin D, a nutrient essential for bone building. However, too much cholesterol in the blood stream is linked to heart disease.

Source: Complete Food and Nutrition Guide, Roberta Larson Duyff, MS, RD, FADA, CFCS.

Fresh fruits and vegetables may be the most important key to good health. They have vitamins, minerals, and lots of different colors and tastes to keep you from getting bored. If you want to be beautiful, smart and sexy, eat more fruits and vegetables!!

Source: James R. Gavin III, MD, PhD; Dr. Gavin's Health Guide.

Quick Tip

The Environmental Working Group (EWG) reports that these 12 items have tested highest among produce for pesticides, so the group suggests we buy organic versions of these foods.

1. celery   2.potatoes   3. lettuce

4.sweet bell peppers   5. spinach   6.strawberries

7.peaches   8.nectarines   9.apples 10.cherries

11.grapes(imported)   12. pears

Source: www.foodnews.org

The Environmental Working Group EWG'S "cleanest 12" list of produce items lowest in pesticides:

1.onions 2.avocado   3.sweetcorn(frozen)

4.pineapples   5.mango 6.sweet peas(frozen)

7.asparagus   8. kiwi   9.bananas   10. cabbage

11. eggplant

Source: www.foodnews.org

   Don't forget:
When buying canned veggies and fruit, look for little or no sodium or added sugar.

When buying dairy products, choose low-fat and no-fat versions.

When buying meat and poultry, go for lean cuts and trim off visible fat.

Source: www.foodnews.org

Quick Tip

IF YOU LOVE: ORANGES, NOW TRY KIWI FRUIT.

This petite fruit contains about 70 milligrams of vitamin C-more than an orange and just 5 milligrams short of the daily recommendation for women. Research links C to improved eyesight, lower cancer risk, and better heart health. All that and a younger-looking outside, too: A high intake of C makes wrinkles less noticeable, according to Melina Jampolis, MD, a San Francisco-based physician who specializes in nutrition and is the author of "The Busy Person's Guide to Permanent Weight Loss."

Bonus: Kiwifruit has 20 percent more potassium than bananas and is one of the few fruits (and veggies) that contain vitamin E.

Source: Health Magazine, July/August 2009.

Quick Tip

A study in Nutrition and Cancer reports that people who regularly consume as little as one and a half servings of soy milk daily enjoy better cancer protection than those who occasionally consume soy. Try to use soy daily, either as soy milk on cereal or oatmeal or as soy protein powder in a fruit smoothie or as a snack of soy nuts. Studies suggest that two separate soy foods a day, in separate meals, work best.

Source: Super Foods Rx; Steven Pratt, M.D; and Kathy Matthews.

Quick Tip

Your toast or cereal could be hiding excessive salt, an additive known to jack up blood pressure. Research says bread and cereal are among the top contributors of sodium to our diet. Getting more than 2,300 mg per day–a mere 1 teaspoonful of tablet salt increases your risk of hypertension. For a heart-healthy morning meal, Dave Grotto, RD, recommends choosing 100% whole grain bread and cereals that contain no more than 150 mg of sodium per serving.

Source: Prevention Magazine, February 2010.

Quick Tip

Carbohydrates-food composed of some combination of starches, sugar and fiber-provide the body with fuel it needs for physical activity by breaking down into glucose, a type of sugar our cells use as a universal energy source.

Bad carbohydrates are foods that have been "stripped" of all bran, fiber, and nutrients. They have been processed in order to make cooking fast and easy.

Examples are white flour and refined sugar, and white rice. They digest so quickly that they cause dramatic elevations in blood sugar, which over time can lead to weight gain, hypoglycemia or even diabetes.

Good carbohydrates are digested more slowly. This keeps your blood sugar and insulin levels from rising and falling too quickly, helping you get full quicker and feel fuller longer. Good sources of carbohydrates include whole grains, beans, fruits, and vegetables, which also offer lots of additional health benefits, including heart disease and cancer prevention.

Source
www.helpguide.org/life/healthy_eating_diet.htm
:

Quick Tip

Avoid or severely limit sugary drinks-they are an easy way to pack calories and chemicals into your diet without even noticing it. One 12-oz soda has about 10 teaspoons of sugar in it! And just because a soda is sugar-free doesn't make it healthy. Recent studies have shown that the artificial sugar substitutes used in soft drinks may interfere with your body's natural regulation system and result in your overindulging in other sweet foods and beverages. Try water with a squeeze of lemon or water with a splash of 100% fruit juice.

Source:
www.helpguide.org/life/healthy_eating_diet.htm

Once again the problem with salt comes with the overuse and over consumption of processed salt most commonly used. It is best to limit sodium to 2,300 mg per day-the equivalent to one teaspoon of salt. Most of the salt in our diets comes from processed, packaged, restaurant, and fast food. Processed food like canned soups or frozen meals can contain hidden sodium that can quickly surpass this recommended amount. Many of us are unaware of how much sodium we are consuming in one day.

Source:
wwvv.helpguide.org/life/healthy_eating_diet.htm

Quick Tip

Eating Shellfish Does Not Increase Heart Disease Risk:

Heart disease is the number-one killer of women, particularly after menopause. High cholesterol increases the risk of heart disease, so many nutritionists recommend reducing cholesterol intake in the diet. Shellfish are high in cholesterol but do not increase the risk of heart disease. A Medical University of South Carolina study showed that middle-aged and older adults who ate large amounts of shellfish had the same risk of heart attack as those eating small amounts. You don't have to give up shrimp, crab or lobster, but go easy on the butter and sauces.

Source: (Journal America Dietetics Association, 109:1422-1426,2009); Fitness Rx, February 2010.

Quick Tip

Visit a local farmer's market. Farmer's markets are springing up all over the U.S. They usually offer a wide variety of products such as fruits, vegetables, flowers, baked goods, eggs, and meat. Small farmers care about their land and the health of their farms, so even if they are not "certified organic" the food they produce is very high quality.

Source:
www.helpguide.org/life/healthy_eating_diet.htm